THE DALAI LAMA'S BOOK OF
TRANSFORMATION

The

DALAI LAMA'S

Book of

TRANSFORMATION

Element
An Imprint of HarperCollins*Publishers*
77–85 Fulham Palace Road,
Hammersmith, London W6 8JB

The website address is: www.thorsonselement.com

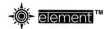

and *Element* are trademarks of
HarperCollins*Publishers* Ltd

First published by Thorsons, an Imprint of
HarperCollins*Publishers* 2000
This edition published by Element 2003

7 9 10 8 6

A catalogue record for this book is
available from the British Library

ISBN 0 00 710097 3

Printed and bound in Great Britain by
Martins The Printers Ltd, Berwick upon Tweed

~

CONTENTS

~

FOREWORD

The Book of Transformation is an extract from the earlier publication of *Transforming the Mind* – teachings by His Holiness the Dalai Lama given in London in May 1999.

It is hoped that this extract – *The Book of Transformation* – will bring His Holiness the Dalai Lama's message about the importance of love, compassion, balanced attitudes and positive thinking to a wider audience.

His Holiness the Dalai Lama is the spiritual and temporal leader of the Tibetan people. In 1989 His Holiness the Dalai Lama was awarded the Nobel

~

Peace Prize for his non-violent struggle for the liberation of Tibet. Since 1959 His Holiness has been living in exile in India. Tibet continues to be occupied by Communist China.

The Office of Tibet, London

June 2000

~

PREFACE

In May 1999 His Holiness the Dalai Lama gave three days' teachings on *The Eight Verses on Transforming the Mind* at the Wembley Conference Centre in London. His Holiness' visit to the United Kingdom took place at the request of the Tibet House Trust, UK.

The Eight Verses on Transforming the Mind is one of the most important texts from a genre of Tibetan spiritual writings known as the *lo-jong*, literally 'transforming the mind.' Written by the eleventh-century Tibetan master Langri Thangpa, this short work is referred to by His Holiness as one of his main sources of inspiration.

~

Central themes of the *lo-jong* teachings include, amongst others, the enhancement of compassion, the cultivation of balanced attitudes towards self and others, the development of positive ways of thinking, and the transformation of adverse situations into conditions favorable to spiritual development.

The Office of Tibet would like to thank Jane Rasch and Cait Collins for transcribing the teachings and Dominique Side for editing. We are grateful to Dr Thupten Jinpa for interpreting His Holiness' teachings into English and also for helping with the editing of the final manuscript.

Mr Migyur Dorjee
Representative of His Holiness the Dalai Lama
in London

PART ONE

THE BASIS OF TRANSFORMATION

~

The whole point of transforming our heart and mind is to find happiness. We all have the natural desire to be happy and the wish to overcome suffering. This is a fact, so we can make it our starting-point.

Before developing this point in more detail, however, let us look very briefly at the nature of experience. Broadly speaking, our experiences fall into two categories. One type of experience is more connected with our bodies, and occurs mainly through our sense organs, while the other type is more related to what can be called 'the mental consciousness' or 'the mind.'

~

~

So far as the physical level of experience is concerned, there is not much difference between ourselves and other animal species. Animals, too, have the capacity to feel both pain and well-being. But what perhaps distinguishes us human beings from other forms of life is that we have far more powerful mental experiences in the form of thoughts and emotions.

~

The fact that there are two broad categories of experience has some interesting implications. Most importantly, if a person's basic state of mind is serene and calm, then it is possible for this inner peace to overwhelm a painful physical experience. On the other hand, if someone is suffering from depression, anxiety, or any form of emotional distress, then even if he or she happens to be enjoying physical comforts, he will not really be able to experience the happiness that these could bring. So this shows that our state of mind, in terms of our attitudes and emotions, plays a crucial role in shaping the way we experience happiness and suffering. The *lo-jong* teachings on transforming the mind offer a series of methods by which we can channel and discipline our mind, and so create the basis for the happiness we are seeking.

~

We all know that there is an intimate connection between physical well-being and emotional well-being. We know, for example, that physical illnesses affect our state of mind, and that, conversely, a greater degree of physical well-being contributes towards greater mental ease. Since we commonly recognize this correlation, many of us engage in physical practices and exercises to help bring about that physical well-being which will contribute to our mental refreshment. There are also certain traditional practices that are aimed at training our energy patterns; these are called *prana yogas*, or 'yogas of the wind energy.' These days, yogic exercises have become very popular in the

~

modern world, too, and this is precisely because many people have found that through yoga they can achieve a degree of physical health that leads to better mental health. The approach that is suggested by the *lo-jong* teachings is slightly different, however. They concentrate directly on the development of the mind itself, through the transformation of our attitudes and ways of thinking.

~

~

The key to transforming our hearts and minds is to have an understanding of the way our thoughts and emotions work. We need to learn how to identify the opposing sides in our inner conflicts. With anger, for example, we need to see how destructive anger is, and, at the same time, realize that there are antidotes within our own thoughts and emotions that we can use to counter it. So, first, by understanding that afflictive thoughts and emotions are destructive and negative, and, second, by trying to strengthen our positive thoughts and emotions, which are their antidotes, we can gradually reduce the force of our anger, hatred and so on.

~

~

The way to examine how thoughts and emotions arise in us is through introspection. It is quite natural for many different thoughts and emotions to arise. When we leave them unexamined and untamed this leads to untold problems, crises, suffering and misery. This is why we need to adopt the conscious discipline we spoke of earlier: in order to reduce the power of a negative emotion like anger or hatred, we need to encourage its anti-dote, which is love and compassion.

~

~

It is not enough to recognize that this is what is required, just as it is not enough simply to wish that love and compassion should increase in us. We have to make a sustained effort, again and again, to cultivate the positive aspects within us, and the key here is constant familiarity. The nature of human thoughts and emotions is such that the more you engage in them, and the more you develop them, the more powerful they become. Therefore we have to develop love and compassion consciously in order to enhance their strength. We are, in fact, talking about a way of cultivating habits that are positive. We do this through meditation.

~

MEDITATION:
A SPIRITUAL DISCIPLINE

What do we understand by meditation? From the Buddhist point of view, meditation is a spiritual discipline, and one that allows you to have some degree of control over your thoughts and emotions.

Why is it that we don't succeed in enjoying the lasting happiness that we are seeking? Buddhism explains that our normal state of mind is such that our thoughts and emotions are wild and unruly, and since we lack the mental discipline needed to tame them, we are powerless to control them. As a result, they control us. And thoughts and

~

emotions, in their turn, tend to be controlled by our negative impulses rather than our positive ones. We need to reverse this cycle.

~

~

The idea of bringing about such a fundamental change in ourselves may at first sight seem impossible, yet it is actually possible to do this through a process of discipline such as meditation. We choose a particular object, and then we train our minds by developing our ability to remain focused on the object. Normally, if we just take a moment to reflect, we will see that our mind is not focused at all. We may be thinking about something and, all of a sudden, we find that we have been distracted because something else came into our head. Our thoughts are constantly chasing after this and that because we don't have the discipline of having a focus. So, through meditation, what we

~

can achieve is the ability to place our minds and to
focus our attention at will on any given object.

~

~

Now of course, we could choose to focus on a negative object in our meditation. If, for example, you are infatuated with someone, and if you focus your mind single-pointedly on that person, and then dwell on their desirable qualities, this will have the effect of increasing your sexual desire for that person. But this is not what meditation is for. From a Buddhist point of view, meditation has to be practiced in relation to a positive object, by which we mean an object that will enhance your ability to focus. Through that familiarity you become closer and closer to the object and feel a sense of intimacy with it. In the classical Buddhist literature this type of meditation is described

~

as *shamatha*, tranquil abiding, which is a single-pointed meditation.

~

~

Shamatha alone is not sufficient. In Buddhism, we combine single-pointed meditation with the practice of analytic meditation, which is known as *vipasyana*, penetrative insight. In this practice we apply reasoning. By recognizing the strengths and weaknesses of different types of emotions and thoughts, together with their advantages and disadvantages, we are able to enhance our positive states of mind which contribute towards a sense of serenity, tranquility, and contentment, and to reduce those attitudes and emotions that lead to suffering and dissatisfaction. Reasoning thus plays a helpful part in this process.

~

~

Whatever forms of meditation you practice, the most important point is to apply mindfulness continuously, and make a sustained effort. It is unrealistic to expect results from meditation within a short period of time. What is required is continuous sustained effort.

~

PART TWO

TRANSFORMING
THROUGH ALTRUISM

~

THE QUALITIES OF
BODHICHITTA, THE ALTRUISTIC
INTENTION

The definition of bodhichitta is given in Maitreya's *Ornament of Realization*, where he states that there are two aspects to altruism. The first is the condition that produces the altruistic outlook, and this involves the compassion that a person must develop towards all sentient beings, and the aspiration he or she must cultivate to bring about the welfare of all sentient beings. This leads to the second aspect, which is the wish to attain

~

enlightenment. It is for the sake of benefitting all beings that this wish should arise in us.

~

~

We could say that bodhichitta is the highest level of altruism and the highest form of courage, and we could also say that bodhichitta is the outcome of the highest altruistic activity. As Lama Tsongkhapa explains in his *Great Exposition of the Path to Enlightenment*, bodhichitta is such that while one engages in fulfilling the wishes of others, the fulfillment of one's own self-interest comes as a by-product. This is a wise way of benefitting both oneself and others. In fact I think bodhichitta is really and truly wonderful. The more I think of helping others, and the stronger my feeling for taking care of others becomes, the more benefit I reap myself. That is quite extraordinary.

~

In a sense we could say that the practice of generating and cultivating the altruistic intention is so comprehensive that it contains the essential elements of all other spiritual practices. Taken alone, it can therefore replace the practice of many different techniques, since all other methods are distilled into one approach. This is why we consider that bodhichitta practice lies at the root of both temporary and lasting happiness. Now the question is how we can train ourselves to develop bodhichitta. The two aspects of bodhichitta that we spoke about earlier, the aspiration to be of help to others and the aspiration to attain enlightenment oneself, have to be cultivated separately

~

through separate trainings. The aspiration to be of help to others has to be cultivated first.

~

~

The Two Altruistic Aspirations

1. The aspiration to attain enlightenment

The highest form of spiritual practice is the cultivation of the altruistic intention to attain enlightenment for the benefit of all sentient beings, known as bodhichitta. This is the most precious state of mind, the supreme source of benefit and goodness, that which fulfills both our immediate and ultimate aspirations, and the basis of altruistic activity. However, bodhichitta can only be realized through regular concerted effort, so in order to attain it we need to cultivate the

~

discipline necessary for training and transforming
our mind.

~

~

As we discussed earlier, the transformation of mind and heart does not happen overnight but through a gradual process. Although it is true that in some cases instantaneous spiritual experiences may be possible, they are rather unreliable and somewhat shortlived. The problem is that when sudden experiences occur, like bolts of lightning, the individual may feel profoundly moved and inspired, but if the experiences are not grounded in discipline and sustained effort they are very unpredictable, and their transformative impact will be rather limited. By contrast, a genuine transformation that results from sustained concerted effort is long-lasting because it has a firm foundation. This is why

~

long-term spiritual transformation can really only
come about through a gradual process of training
and discipline.

~

The potential for perfection, the potential for full enlightenment, actually lies within each one of us. In fact this potential is nothing other than the essential nature of the mind itself, which is said to be the mere nature of luminosity and knowing. Through the gradual process of spiritual practice, we can eliminate the obstructions that hinder us from perfecting this seed of enlightenment. As we overcome them, step by step, so the inherent quality of our consciousness begins to become more and more manifest until it reaches the highest stage of perfection, which is none other than the enlightened mind of the Buddha.

2. Working for the welfare of others

The other aspiration of the altruistic intention (bodhichitta) is the wish to bring about the welfare of other sentient beings. Welfare, in the Buddhist sense, means helping others to attain total freedom from suffering, and the term 'other sentient beings' refers to the infinite number of beings in the universe. This aspiration is really the key to the first, namely the intention to attain enlightenment for the benefit of all sentient beings. It is founded on genuine compassion towards all sentient beings equally. Compassion here means the wish that all other beings should be free of suffering. So it is

~

said to be at the root of all altruistic activity and of the altruistic intention as a whole.

~

~

We need to cultivate a compassion that is powerful enough to make us feel committed to bringing about the well-being of others, so that we are actually willing to shoulder the responsibility for making this happen. In Buddhism, such compassion is called 'great compassion.' The point is emphasized again and again that great compassion is the foundation of all positive qualities, the root of the entire Mahayana path, and the heart of bodhichitta. Likewise, Chandrakirti says in his *Entry to the Middle Way* that compassion is such a supreme spiritual quality that it maintains its relevance at all times: it is vital at the initial stage of the spiritual path, it is just as important while

~

we are on the path, and it is equally relevant when an individual has become fully enlightened.

~

~

Generally speaking, as I said, compassion is the wish that others should be free of suffering, but if we look into it more closely compassion has two levels. In one case it may exist simply at the level of a wish – just wishing the other to be free of suffering – but it can also exist on a higher level, where the emotion goes beyond a mere wish to include the added dimension of actually wanting to do something about the suffering of others. In this case, a sense of responsibility and personal commitment enters into the thought and emotion of altruism.

~

~

Whichever level of compassion we may have, for the development of bodhichitta to be successful it must be combined with the complementary factor of wisdom and insight. If you lack wisdom and insight, when you are confronted with another's suffering, genuine compassion may arise in you spontaneously, but given that your resources are limited, you may only be able to make a wish: 'May he or she be free of that pain or suffering.' However, over time that kind of feeling may lead to a feeling of helplessness because you realize you cannot really do anything to change the situation. On the other hand, if you are equipped with wisdom and insight then you have a much greater

~

resource to draw on, and the more you focus on the object of compassion, the greater the intensity of your compassion will be and the more it will increase.

~

~

Because of the way insight and wisdom affect the development of compassion, the Buddhist literature identifies three different types of compassion. First, at the initial stage, compassion is simply the wish to see other sentient beings freed from suffering; it is not reinforced by any particular insight into the nature of suffering or the nature of a sentient being. Then, at the second stage, compassion is not simply the wish to see another being free from suffering, it is strengthened by insight into the transient nature of existence, such as the realization that the being who is the object of your compassion does not exist permanently. When insight complements your compassion it gives it

~

greater power. Finally, at the third stage, compassion is described as 'non-objectifying compassion.' It can be directed towards that same suffering being, but now it is reinforced by a full awareness of the ultimate nature of that being. This is a very powerful type of compassion, because it enables you to engage with the other person without objectifying him or her, and without clinging on to the idea that he or she has any absolute reality.

~

~

Since compassion is the wish that others should be free of suffering, it requires above all the ability to feel connected to other beings. We know from experience that the closer we feel towards a particular person or animal, the greater our capacity to empathize with that being. It follows, then, that an important element in the spiritual practice of developing compassion is the ability to feel empathetic and connected, and to have a sense of closeness with others. Buddhism describes this as a sense of intimacy with the object of compassion; it is also called loving-kindness. The closer you feel towards another being, the more powerfully you will feel that the sight of his or her suffering is unbearable.

~

There are two main methods in Buddhism for cultivating this sense of closeness or intimacy. One is the method known as 'exchanging and equalizing oneself with others.' Although it stems from Nagarjuna, it was more fully developed by Shantideva in his *Guide to the Bodhisattva's Way of Life* (Bodhicaryavatara). The other technique is known as the 'seven-point cause and effect method.' This emphasizes the cultivation of an attitude that enables us to relate to all other beings as we would to someone very dear. The traditional example given is that we should consider all sentient beings as our mother, but some scriptures also include considering beings as our father, or as

~

dear friends, or as close relatives, and so on. Our mother is simply taken as an example, but the point is that we should learn to view all other sentient beings as very dear and close to our hearts.

~

~

It seems that for some the seven-point cause and effect method is more effective, while for others the technique of exchanging and equalizing self with others appears to be more effective, depending upon the individual's inclinations and mentality. However, within the Tibetan tradition the custom really has been to combine both these methods so that one can enjoy the benefits of practicing both approaches.

~

~

The Seven-Point Cause and Effect Method

The seven points are: recognizing that all sentient beings have been our mother in a past life; reflecting on the kindness of all beings; meditating on repaying their kindness; meditating on love; meditating on compassion; generating the extraordinary attitude of universal responsibility; and the actual development of bodhichitta.

Before we can apply the seven-point cause and effect method to ourselves, we need to cultivate a sense of equanimity towards all sentient beings, which is expressed through the ability to relate to

~

all others equally. To do this, we need to address the problem of having thoughts and emotions that fluctuate. Not only should we try to overcome extreme negative emotions like anger and hatred, but also, in this particular spiritual practice, we should try to work with the attachment we feel to our loved ones.

~

~

Now, of course, in this attachment to loved ones there is a sense of closeness and intimacy, as well as an element of love, compassion and affection, but often these emotions are also tinged with a strong feeling of desire. The reason for that is rather obvious, because when we relate to people towards whom we feel deeply attached, our feelings are highly susceptible to emotional extremes. When such a person does something that is contrary to our expectations, for instance, it has a much greater potential to hurt us than if the same thing were done by someone to whom we do not feel that close. This indicates that in the affection we feel there is a high degree of attachment. So, in

~

this particular spiritual practice, we try to level out
the attachment we have to certain people, so that
our sense of closeness to them is genuine and not
tinged with desire.

~

~

The key point in this preliminary practice of equanimity is to overcome the feelings of partiality and discrimination that we normally feel towards others, based on the fluctuating emotions and thoughts associated with closeness and distance. It really seems to be true that attachment constrains our vision, so that we are not able to see things from a wider perspective.

~

~

Recently I was at a seminar on science and religion in Argentina, and one of the participant scientists made a point which I think is very true. He said that it is very important for research scientists to adopt the methodological principle of not being emotionally attached to their field of inquiry. This is because attachment has the negative effect of clouding and narrowing your vision. I totally agree. This is why, through the practice of equanimity, we try to overcome these feelings of partiality so that we can deal with everything and relate to everyone even-handedly.

~

~

When we practice developing equanimity, sometimes it is helpful to use visualization. For example, you can imagine three different individuals in front of you: someone who is very close to you, someone you regard as an enemy and whom you dislike, and then someone who is completely neutral and to whom you feel indifferent. Then let your natural emotions and thoughts arise in relation to these three individuals. Once you are able to allow your natural feelings to arise, you will notice that towards the loved one you feel a sense of closeness and also great attachment, towards the person you dislike you may feel hostility and a sense of distance, and that towards

~

the individual who is neutral you will hardly feel
any emotion at all.

~

~

At this point, try to reason with yourself. 'Why do I feel such different emotions towards these three individuals? Why do I feel so attached to my loved ones?' You might begin to see that there are certain grounds for your attachment: the person is dear to you because he or she has done this and that for you, and so on. But if you then ask yourself whether these characteristics are permanent and whether the person will always be like this, then you may have to concede that this is not necessarily the case. Someone may be a friend today but turn into an enemy tomorrow. This is especially true from the Buddhist point of view, when we take many lifetimes into account –

~

someone who is very close to you in this life may have been your enemy in another. From this perspective there are no real grounds for feeling such strong attachment.

~

~

In the same way, then turn your attention towards the person you dislike and ask yourself, 'On what grounds do I feel such negative emotions towards this person?' Again, this may be because he or she has done certain things towards you. But then ask yourself whether that person is likely to remain your enemy all his life. And then, if you take into account the question of many lifetimes, you will realize that the individual may have been very close to you in a past life, so his status as your enemy is merely short term. You begin to see that there are no justifiable grounds for having such extreme hatred and anger towards that person.

~

Finally, consider the individual in the middle, to whom you feel totally indifferent. If you raise the same kind of questions again, you will realize that the person may have very little relevance to your present life but may have been important to you in other lives in the past; and even in this lifetime, he may become important to you at some future point. So this type of visualization helps to level out the extreme fluctuating emotions that you feel towards others, and to establish a stable basis on which you can build a more balanced sense of closeness. If we think along these lines, and question our emotions from various angles, then we come to appreciate that the extreme emotions that

~

we tend to feel towards others, and the behaviors they generate, are perhaps unwise.

~

Thinking of Others as Someone Dear

Having developed equanimity, we can begin the
first stage of the seven-point practice, which is
cultivating the attitude of thinking of all others as
being as dear to you as your mother, or father, or
friend. Here, of course, the teachings take into
account the idea of beginningless lifetimes, so all
other sentient beings are considered to have been
our mother or father or friend at one point or
another. This is the way we try to relate to others
and to develop a genuine sense of connection.

~

The reason this practice is traditionally considered so important is because, in nature, it is predominantly mothers who play the most critical role in nurturing and bringing up their offspring. In some animal species both mother and father remain together to look after their young, but in most cases it is just the mother. There are some exceptions, of course. There are some species of bird where the mother hardly participates at all in the building of the nest; it is the male that works hard to build the nest while the female just looks on and inspects the result! It then seems quite fair that the male takes greater responsibility in the nurturing process. However, such cases are rare.

~

It is for these reasons that traditional Indian and Tibetan texts single out mothers as an example of how we should relate to other beings. In fact the Tibetan language has coined a special term for 'dear old mother sentient beings,' and the expression has become so deeply embedded in people's psyche, it has a poetic ring to it. Nowadays, whenever people raise gender issues in the context of Tibetan culture, I tell them that for me the whole idea of 'mother sentient beings,' and the Tibetan expression that goes with it, is a good example of how motherhood was valued in Buddhist culture.

~

In the traditional literature, it is understood that this profound recognition of all sentient beings as being like one's mother is based upon the notion of successive lifetimes, so the whole question of rebirth and past lives comes into the picture here. The Buddhist teachings emphasize the need to understand the possibility of rebirth on the basis of understanding the nature of consciousness. The point is made that consciousness is a phenomenon that arises due only to a previous moment of consciousness. Matter cannot become consciousness. As regards the connection between mind and matter generally, one can contribute towards the causation of the other, but in terms of an

~

individual continuum, consciousness must be caused by a preceding moment of consciousness.

~

~

Reflecting on the Kindness of All Beings

The second element of the seven-point cause and effect method is reflecting upon the kindness of all beings. In your meditation, you focus on the kindness of others, especially in the context that they have been your mother in this or other lifetimes, and this naturally leads to the thought, 'I must repay their kindness. I must acknowledge the profound kindness they have shown to me.' Such feelings will arise naturally in someone who is honorable, ethical, and what we could call 'civilized.'

~

~

Once you recognize all other beings as your kind, dear mothers then naturally you will feel close to them. With this as a basis, you should cultivate love or loving-kindness, which is traditionally defined as the wish to see others enjoy happiness, and then you also develop compassion, which is the wish for others to be free of suffering. Love and compassion are two sides of the same coin.

~

~

Exchanging and Equalizing Oneself with Others

We will now turn to the other method for transforming the mind, which is exchanging and equalizing oneself with others. Here again, the first stage is the cultivation of equanimity, although the meaning of equanimity in this context is different from the one we spoke of earlier. Here, equanimity is understood as the fundamental equality of all beings, in the sense that just as you have the spontaneous wish to be happy and overcome suffering, so does every single other being, in equal measure.

~

Now we try to probe deeper to understand what this aspiration to be free of suffering really implies. It does not arise from a sense of self-importance, or self-congratulation; such considerations simply do not play any role here at all. This basic aspiration arises in us simply by virtue of the fact that we are conscious living beings. Together with this aspiration comes a conviction that I, as an individual, have a legitimate right to fulfill my aspiration. If we accept this, then we can relate the same principle to others and we will realize that everyone else shares this basic aspiration too. Therefore, if I as an individual have the right to fulfill my aspiration, then others, too, have an equal right to fulfill

~

theirs. It is on these grounds that one has to recognize the fundamental equality of all beings.

~

~

Within the practice of equalizing and exchanging oneself with others, this is the equalizing stage, where we develop the understanding that we and others are fundamentally equal. The next stage involves reflecting on the shortcomings of excessively self-cherishing thoughts, and their negative consequences, as well as reflecting on the merits of developing thoughts that cherish the well-being of others.

~

~

How do we do this? We begin by comparing ourselves with others. We have accepted that there is a fundamental equality between ourselves and others in terms of our respective aspirations to be happy and overcome suffering, and we have also recognized that all beings, including ourselves, have an equal right to fulfill that aspiration. No matter how important an individual person may be, and no matter how unimportant, in a worldly sense, others may be, so far as the basic fact of wishing to be happy and overcome suffering is concerned, there is absolute equality. So what is the difference between us? The difference is really a matter of numbers. No matter how important an

~

individual is, the interest of that individual is the interest of only one being, whereas the interest of others is the interest of an infinite number of beings.

~

The question is, which is more important? Simply from the numerical point of view, if we want to be fair we have to accept that the interest of others is more important than our own. Even in the mundane world we know that the issues which affect the lives of many people are generally granted greater significance than those that affect fewer people or a single individual. So, logically, one has to accept that the well-being of others is more important than one's own. To be completely rational or objective, one could say that sacrificing the interest of the many for the sake of one person is an unwise and foolish act, whereas sacrificing the interest of one individual for the benefit of an

~

infinite number of others is more rational, if such
a choice is necessary.

~

~

Now, you might think that all of this sounds fine, but at the end of the day you are 'you' and others are 'other.' If self and others are totally independent of each other, and there is no connection whatsoever between them, then perhaps there is a case for ignoring the well-being of others and simply pursuing one's own self-interest. However, this is not the case. Self and others are not really independent; in fact, their respective interests are intertwined.

~

~

From the Buddhist point of view, even when you are unenlightened your life is so intertwined with those of others that you cannot really carve yourself out as a single isolated individual. Also, when you follow a spiritual path, many spiritual realizations depend on your interaction with others, so here again others are indispensable. Even when you have attained the highest state of enlightenment, your enlightened activities are for the benefit of others. Indeed, enlightened activity comes about spontaneously by virtue of the fact that other beings exist, so others are indispensable even at that stage. Your life and the lives of others are so interconnected that the idea of a self that is

~

totally distinct and independent of others really
does not make any sense.

~

~

Although this is the reality, it is not reflected in our behavior. Until now, regardless of reality, we have nurtured within ourselves a whole complex of self-cherishing thoughts. We believe in something that we hold very dear and we regard as precious, something that is like the core of our being; and this is accompanied by a powerful belief in our existence as an individual being with an independent reality. The belief that there is a substantially real self, and the cherishing of one's own interest at the expense of others, are the two main thoughts and emotions we have nurtured within us throughout our many lives. But what is the result of this? What benefit does it bring? We are

~

continually suffering, we are continually experiencing negative thoughts and emotions, so our self-cherishing hasn't really got us very far.

~

~

If we shift our focus from ourselves to others and to the wider world, and if we turn our attention to all the crises in the world, all the difficulties and the sufferings and so on, we will see that many of these problems are direct or indirect consequences of undisciplined negative states of mind. And where do these come from? From this powerful combination of self-centeredness and the belief in our independent existence. By shifting our attention to the wider world in this way, we can begin to appreciate the immensely destructive consequences of such thinking.

~

~

These attitudes are not helpful even from one's own selfish point of view. We might ask ourselves, 'What benefit do I as an individual derive from my self-centeredness, and from the belief in my existence as an independent self?' When you really think deeply, you will realize the answer is 'Not very much.'

~

~

In fact, these beliefs are the source of suffering and misery even for the individual. The Buddhist literature is full of discussions on this. Interestingly, about two years ago, I was at a medical conference in America, and a participating psychologist presented the findings of research he had carried out over a long period of time. One conclusion he considered almost indisputable was that there seems to be a correlation between early death, high blood pressure and heart disease on one side, and a disproportionately high use of first personal pronouns on the other ('I', 'me,' and 'mine'). I thought this finding was very interesting. Even scientific studies seem to suggest that there is a

~

correlation between excessive self-cherishing and damage to one's physical well-being.

~

~

Now in contrast, if you shift your focus from yourself to others, extend your concern to others, and cultivate the thought of caring for the well-being of others, then this will have the immediate effect of opening up your life and helping you to reach out. In other words, the practice of cultivating altruism has a beneficial effect not only from the religious point of view but also from the mundane point of view, not only for long-term spiritual development but even in terms of immediate rewards. From my own personal experience I can tell you that when I practice altruism and care for others, it immediately makes me calmer and more secure. So altruism brings immediate benefits.

~

The same applies when you cultivate the understanding that the self is not really an independently existing entity, and begin to view self instead in terms of its dependent relation to others. Although it is difficult to say that merely reflecting on this will produce a profound spiritual realization, it will at least have some effect. Your mind will be more open. Something will begin to change within you. Therefore, even in the immediate term there is definitely a positive and beneficial effect in reversing these two attitudes and moving from self-centeredness to other-centeredness, from belief in self-existence to belief in dependent origination.

~

~

To summarize, I agree with Shantideva when he
writes:

What need is there to say more?
The childish work for their own benefit,
The buddhas work for the benefit of others.
Just look at the difference between them.

If I do not exchange my happiness
For the suffering of others,
I shall not attain the state of buddhahood
And even in samsara I shall have no real joy.

~

The source of all misery in the world

Lies in thinking of oneself;

The source of all happiness

Lies in thinking of others.

~

PART THREE

TRANSFORMATION
THROUGH INSIGHT

~

INSIGHT INTO THE NATURE OF
SUFFERING

Along with the methods for cultivating a sense of closeness to others there is another key element for developing compassion, and that is deepening our insight into the nature of suffering. The Tibetan tradition maintains that contemplation on suffering is much more effective when it is done on the basis of one's own personal experience, and when it is focused on oneself, because, generally, we tend to be better able to relate to our own suffering than to that of others. This is why two of the principal elements of the Buddhist path, compassion

~

and renunciation, are seen as two sides of the same coin. True renunciation arises when one has a genuine insight into the nature of suffering, focused upon oneself, and true compassion arises when that focus shifts to others; so the difference lies simply in the object of focus.

~

~

So far as the first level of suffering is concerned – physical pain and other obvious sufferings – we consider that even animals have the capacity to recognize these experiences as suffering, and they are also capable of finding relief from some aspect of them, however temporary that may be. As for the suffering of change, which is the second category, this actually refers to experiences that we conventionally identify as pleasurable or happy. These are subject to the suffering of change, because the more you indulge in them, the more they lead to dissatisfaction. If these experiences were bringing some genuine lasting happiness, then the more you indulged in them the longer the experience of

~

happiness would last, yet that is not the case. All too often what may seem like a pleasurable experience, and what may initially seem like happiness, when pursued, changes at a certain point into suffering and leads to frustration and so on. So even though conventionally it is called happiness, in another sense it has the nature of suffering. In fact, if you examine the nature of pleasurable sensations you will see that there is often an extremely relative dimension to them; we usually define an experience as pleasurable by comparison to a more intense form of suffering that has just come to an end. What we call 'pleasure' or 'happiness' is more like the temporary absence of intense suffering and pain.

~

However, this is not the deeper meaning of suffering that we speak about in Buddhism. The suffering of change is identified as a type of suffering by many other spiritual traditions, too, and there are methods that are common to both Buddhist and non-Buddhist Indian traditions that allow the individual to recognize these experiences as suffering and to gain temporary freedom from it. These methods include various meditative techniques, the cultivation of absorptive states of mind, contemplations, and so on.

~

It is the third level of suffering, called 'the suffering of pervasive conditioning,' that we are concerned with here. The suffering of conditioning is the origin of the other two types of suffering. It is the nature of our very existence, which comes about as a result of karma, delusions, and afflictive emotions. Our very existence as unenlightened beings is said to be fundamentally unsatisfactory, or duhkha, that is, suffering. Through the practice of compassion and renunciation, we need to develop a genuine desire to gain freedom from this third level of suffering, but this desire can only arise if we understand the nature of suffering and its causes.

~

When you engage in deep contemplation on the nature of suffering, on the causes of suffering, and on the fact that there exist powerful antidotes to those causes, and when you reflect on the possibility of freedom from suffering and its causes, then you will be able to develop genuine renunciation from the depths of your heart, for you will truly aspire to gain freedom from suffering. At this stage, you will have a sense of being completely exhausted by your experience of unenlightened existence, and by the fact that you are under the domination of negative thoughts and emotions.

~

~

After you establish the aspiration to gain freedom from that kind of existence, you can shift that aspiration to others, and focus on others' experience of suffering, which is the same as your own. If you combine that with the reflections we mentioned earlier – recognizing all sentient beings as dear mothers, reflecting upon their kindness, and realizing the fundamental equality of oneself and others – then there is a real possibility for genuine compassion to arise within you. Only then will you have the genuine aspiration to be of benefit to others.

~

PART FOUR

THE EIGHT VERSES
ON TRANSFORMING
THE MIND

~

Until now, we have talked about the basis that makes spiritual transformation possible, and about the need for training the mind. The most essential point is the development of bodhichitta, the altruistic intention to attain enlightenment for the sake of all sentient beings, which arises from training in the two aspirations. As a means to enhance our practice it is advised that we should constantly apply it in our daily life, and to our behavior as a whole – physical, verbal, and mental. Verbal action includes reading texts like The Eight Verses on Transforming the Mind, presented here as an aid to constantly remind you of the importance of undertaking this kind of contemplation.

~

The development of bodhichitta is the core of the Buddha's teaching, and the main path. Once the development of bodhichitta has taken place, the practitioner endeavors to apply the altruistic principle throughout his or her life. This leads to what are known as the 'bodhisattva ideals,' including the 'six perfections' – the perfections of generosity, morality, patience, enthusiasm, meditation or concentration, and wisdom.

~

~

The point I wish to make here is that the practice of compassion is at the heart of the entire path. All other practices are either preliminary to it, or a foundation for it, or they are subsequent applications of this core practice. I would also like to point out that there is a consensus between all Buddhist schools on this, in both Mahayana and non-Mahayana traditions. So compassion lies at the root of all the Buddha's teaching, but it is within the bodhisattva ideal that we find special emphasis on the concerted development of compassion by means of cultivating bodhichitta.

~

~

THE EIGHT VERSES ON
TRANSFORMING THE MIND

With a determination to achieve the highest aim
For the benefit of all sentient beings,
Which surpasses even the wish-fulfilling gem,
May I hold them dear at all times.

In this verse you are making the aspiration to hold all other sentient beings as supremely dear to you, because they are the basis upon which you can achieve the highest goal, which is the welfare of sentient beings. This goal surpasses even the legendary wish-fulfilling jewel, because however

~

precious such a jewel may be, it cannot provide the highest spiritual attainment. There is also a reference here to the kindness of all other beings, and we spoke of the meaning of this earlier. It is due to other sentient beings that you can develop great compassion, the highest spiritual principle, and it is thanks to other sentient beings that you can develop bodhichitta, the altruistic intention. So it is on the basis of your interaction with others that you can attain the highest spiritual realizations. From that point of view, the kindness of others is very profound.

~

When we talk of cultivating the thought of holding others as supremely dear, it is important to understand that we are not cultivating the kind of pity that we sometimes feel towards someone who is less fortunate than ourselves. With pity, there can be a tendency to look down upon the object of our compassion, and to feel a sense of superiority. Holding others dear is in fact the reverse of this. In this practice, by recognizing the kindness of others and how indispensable they are for our own spiritual progress, we appreciate their tremendous importance and significance, and therefore we naturally accord them a higher status in our minds. It is because we think of them in this way that we

~

are able to relate to them as dear, and as worthy of our respect and affection. Because of this, the next verse reads:

~

~

Whenever I interact with someone,

May I view myself as the lowest amongst all,

And, from the very depths of my heart,

Respectfully hold others as superior.

This verse suggests the kind of attitude that I have just described. The idea of seeing oneself as lower than others should not be misconstrued as a way of neglecting ourselves, ignoring our needs, or feeling that we are a hopeless case. Rather, as I explained earlier, it stems from a courageous state of mind where you are able to relate to others, fully aware of what ability you have to help. So please do not misunderstand this point.

~

What is being suggested here is the need for genuine humility.

~

~

I would like to tell a story to illustrate this. There was a great master about two or three generations ago called Dza Patrul Rinpoche. Not only was he a great master but he had a large following, and he would often give teachings to thousands of students. But he was also a meditator, so occasionally he would disappear to do a retreat somewhere, and his students would have to run around to search for him. During one of these breaks he was on a pilgrimage, and he stayed for a couple of days with a family, like many Tibetan pilgrims did; they would seek shelter with a family on the road and do some chores in return for food. So Dza Patrul Rinpoche did various chores for the family,

~

including emptying the mother's potty, which he
did on a regular basis.

~

~

Eventually some of his students arrived in that region, and heard that Dza Patrul Rinpoche was somewhere around, and a number of monks finally reached this household and approached the mother of the house. 'Do you know where Dza Patrul Rinpoche is?' they asked. 'I don't know of any Dza Patrul Rinpoche around here,' she replied. The monks then described him to her, and added, 'We heard he was living in your house as a pilgrim.' 'Oh,' she cried, 'that is Dza Patrul Rinpoche!' Apparently, just at that moment, Dza Patrul Rinpoche had gone to empty her potty. The mother was so horrified that she ran away!

~

~

What this story tells us is that even in a great lama like Dza Patrul Rinpoche, who had a following of thousands, and who was used to giving teachings from a high throne, surrounded by many monks, and so on, there was a genuine humility. He had no hesitation when it came to doing a chore like emptying the potty of an elderly lady.

~

~

There are particular ways in which one can practice viewing oneself as lower than others. To take a simple example, we all know from experience that when we focus on a particular object or individual, according to the angle from which we view it, we will have a different perspective. This is, in fact, the nature of thought. Thoughts are capable of selecting only isolated characteristics of a given object at a particular time, human thought is not capable of comprehensively viewing something in its entirety. The nature of thought is to be selective. When you realize this, you can view yourself as lower than others from a certain point of view, even in comparison to a tiny insect.

~

Let's say that I compare myself to an insect. I am a
follower of the Buddha, and a human being
equipped with the capacity to think and, suppos-
edly, to be able to judge between right and wrong.
I am also supposed to have some knowledge of the
fundamental teachings of the Buddha, and theo-
retically I am committed to these practices. Yet
when I find certain negative tendencies arising in
me, or when I carry out negative actions on the
basis of these impulses, then from that point of
view there is certainly a case to be made that I am
in some ways inferior to the insect. After all, an
insect is not able to judge between right and
wrong in the way humans can, it has no capacity to

~

think in a long-term way and is unable to understand the intricacies of spiritual teachings, so from
the Buddhist point of view, whatever an insect
does is the result of habituation and karma. By
comparison, human beings have the ability to
determine what they do. If, despite this, we act
negatively then it could be argued that we are inferior to that innocent insect! So when you think
along these lines, there are genuine grounds for
seeing ourselves as inferior to all other sentient
beings.

~

~

The third verse reads:

In all my deeds may I probe into my mind,
And as soon as mental and emotional afflictions arise –
As they endanger myself and others –
May I strongly confront them and avert them.

This indicates that although all of us, as spiritual practitioners, wish to overcome our negative impulses, thoughts and emotions, owing to our long habituation to negative tendencies, and to our lack of diligence in applying the necessary antidotes to them, afflictive emotions and thoughts do occur in us spontaneously and quite powerfully.

~

Such is their force, in fact, that we are often driven by these negative tendencies. This verse suggests we should be aware of this fact so that we remain alert. We should constantly check ourselves and take note when negative tendencies arise in us, so that we can catch them as they arise. If we do this then we will not give in to them; we will be able to remain on our guard and keep a certain distance from them. In this way we won't reinforce them, and we will be spared from undergoing an explosion of strong emotion and the negative words and actions to which that leads.

~

~

But generally, this is not what happens. Even if we know that negative emotions are destructive, if they are not very intense we tend to think, 'Oh, maybe this one is OK.' We tend to treat them rather casually. The problem is that the longer you are accustomed to the afflictions within you, the more prone you become to their reoccurring, and then the greater your propensity will be to give in to them. This is how negativity perpetuates itself. So it is important to be mindful, as the text urges, so that whenever afflictive emotions arise you are able to confront them and avert them immediately.

~

~

It is very important, especially for a Buddhist practitioner, to constantly check oneself in daily life, to check one's thoughts and feelings even, if possible, during one's dreams. As you train yourself in the application of mindfulness, gradually you will be able to apply it more and more regularly, and its effectiveness as a tool will increase.

~

~

The next verse reads:

When I see beings of unpleasant character
Oppressed by strong negativity and suffering,
May I hold them dear – for they are rare to find –
As if I have discovered a jewel treasure!

This verse refers to the special case of relating to people who are socially marginalized, perhaps because of their behavior, their appearance, their destitution, or on account of some illness. Whoever practices bodhichitta must take special care of these people, as if, on meeting them, you have found a real treasure. Instead of feeling

~

repulsed, a true practitioner of these altruistic principles should engage and take on the challenge of relating. In fact, the way we interact with people of this kind could give a great impetus to our spiritual practice.

~

~

I am glad to say that I've heard that some Buddhist centers are beginning to apply Buddhist principles socially. For example, I have heard of Buddhist centers involved in some form of spiritual education in prisons, where they give talks and offer counseling. I think this is a great example. It is of course deeply unfortunate when such people, particularly prisoners, feel rejected by society. Not only is it deeply painful for them, but also, from a broader point of view, it is a loss for society. We are not providing the opportunity for these people to make a constructive social contribution when they actually have the potential to do so. I therefore think it is important for society as a whole not to

~

reject such individuals, but to embrace them and acknowledge the potential contribution they can make. In this way they will feel they have a place in society, and will begin to think that they might perhaps have something to offer.

~

~

The next verse reads:

When others, out of jealously
Treat me wrongly with abuse, slander, and scorn,
May I take upon myself the defeat
And offer to others the victory.

The point that is made here is that when others provoke you, perhaps for no reason or unjustly, instead of reacting in a negative way, as a true practitioner of altruism you should be able to be tolerant towards them. You should remain unperturbed by such treatment. In the next verse we learn that not only should we be tolerant of such

~

people, but in fact we should view them as our spiritual teachers. It reads:

~

~

When someone whom I have helped,

Or in whom I have placed great hopes,

Mistreats me in extremely hurtful ways,

May I regard him still as my precious teacher.

In Shantideva's *Guide to the Bodhisattva's Way of Life*, there is an extensive discussion of how we can develop this kind of attitude, and how we can actually learn to see those who perpetrate harm on us as objects of spiritual learning. And also, in the third chapter of Chandrakirti's *Entry to the Middle Way*, there are profoundly inspiring and effective teachings on the cultivation of patience and tolerance.

~

The seventh verse summarizes all the practices
that we have been discussing. It reads:

In brief, may I offer benefit and joy
To all my mothers, both directly and indirectly,
May I quietly take upon myself
All hurts and pains of my mothers.

This verse presents a specific Buddhist practice
known as 'the practice of giving and taking' (*tong
len*), and it is by means of the visualization of
giving and taking that we practice equalizing and
exchanging ourselves with others.

~

~

'Exchanging ourselves with others' should not be taken in the literal sense of turning oneself into the other and the other into oneself. This is impossible anyway. What is meant here is a reversal of the attitudes one normally has towards oneself and others. We tend to relate to this so-called 'self' as a precious core at the center of our being, something that is really worth taking care of, to the extent that we are willing to overlook the well-being of others. In contrast, our attitude towards others often resembles indifference; at best we may have some concern for them, but even this may simply remain at the level of a feeling or an emotion. On the whole we are indifferent towards

~

others' well-being and do not take it seriously. So the point of this particular practice is to reverse this attitude so that we reduce the intensity of our grasping and the attachment we have to ourselves, and endeavor to consider the well-being of others as significant and important.

~

~

When approaching Buddhist practices of this kind, where there is a suggestion that we should take harm and suffering upon ourselves, I think it is vital to consider them carefully and appreciate them in their proper context. What is actually being suggested here is that if, in the process of following your spiritual path and learning to think about the welfare of others, you are led to take on certain hardships or even suffering, then you should be totally prepared for this. The texts do not imply that you should hate yourself, or be harsh on yourself, or somehow wish misery upon yourself in a masochistic way. It is important to know that this is not the meaning.

~

Another example we should not misinterpret is the verse in a famous Tibetan text which reads, 'May I have the courage if necessary to spend aeons and aeons, innumerable lifetimes, even in the deepest hell realm.' The point that is being made here is that the level of your courage should be such that if this is required of you as part of the process of working for others' well-being, then you should have the willingness and commitment to accept it.

~

~

A correct understanding of these passages is very important, because otherwise you may use them to reinforce any feelings of self-hatred, thinking that if the self is the embodiment of self-centeredness, one should banish oneself into oblivion. Do not forget that ultimately the motivation behind wishing to follow a spiritual path is to attain supreme happiness, so just as one seeks happiness for oneself one is also seeking happiness for others. Even from a practical point of view, for someone to develop genuine compassion towards others, first he or she must have a basis upon which to cultivate compassion, and that basis is the ability to connect to one's own feelings and to care for one's

~

own welfare. If one is not capable of doing that, how can one reach out to others and feel concern for them? Caring for others requires caring for oneself. The practice of *tong len*, giving and taking, encapsulates the practices of loving-kindness and compassion: the practice of giving emphasizes the practice of loving-kindness, where-as the practice of taking emphasizes the practice of compassion.

~

~

Shantideva suggests an interesting way of doing this practice in his *Guide to the Bodhisattva's Way of Life*. It is a visualization to help us appreciate the shortcomings of self-centeredness, and provide us with methods to confront it. On one side you visualize your own normal self, the self that is totally impervious to others' well-being and an embodiment of self-centeredness. This is the self that only cares about its own well-being, to the extent that it is often willing to exploit others quite arrogantly to reach its own ends. Then, on the other side, you visualize a group of beings who are suffering, with no protection and no refuge. You can focus your attention on specific individuals if

~

you wish. For example, if you wish to visualize someone you know well and care about, and who is suffering, then you can take that person as a specific object of your visualization and do the entire practice of giving and taking in relation to him or her. Thirdly, you view yourself as a neutral third person or impartial observer, who tries to assess whose interest is more important here. Isolating yourself in the position of neutral observer makes it easier for you to see the limitations of self-centeredness, and realize how much fairer and more rational it is to concern yourself with the welfare of other sentient beings.

~

~

As a result of this visualization, you slowly begin to feel an affinity with others and a deep empathy with their suffering, and at this point you can begin the actual meditation of giving and taking.

~

~

    In order to carry out the meditation on taking, it is often quite helpful to do another visualization. First, you focus your attention on suffering beings, and try to develop and intensify your compassion towards them, to the point where you feel that their suffering is almost unbearable. At the same time, however, you realize that there is not much you can do to help them in a practical sense. So in order to train yourself to become more effective, with a compassionate motivation you visualize taking upon yourself their suffering, the causes of their suffering, their negative thoughts and emotions, and so forth. You can do this by imagining all their suffering and negativity as a stream of

~

dark smoke, and you visualize this smoke dissolving into you. In the context of this practice you can also visualize sharing your own positive qualities with others. You can think of any meritorious actions that you have done, any positive potential that may lie in you, and also any spiritual knowledge or insight that you may have attained. You send them out to other sentient beings, so that they too can enjoy their benefits. You can do this by imagining your qualities in the form of either a bright light or a whitish stream of light, which penetrates other beings and is absorbed into them. This is how to practice the visualization of taking and giving.

~

Of course, this kind of meditation will not have a material effect on others because it is a visualization, but what it can do is help increase your concern for others and your empathy with their suffering, while also helping to reduce the power of your self-centeredness. These are the benefits of the practice. This is how you train your mind to cultivate the altruistic aspiration to help other sentient beings. When this arises together with the aspiration to attain full enlightenment, then you have realized bodhichitta, that is, the altruistic intention to become fully enlightened for the sake of all sentient beings.

~

~

In the final verse, we read:

May all this remain undefiled
By the stains of the eight mundane concerns;
And may I, recognizing all things as illusion,
Devoid of clinging, be released from bondage.

The first two lines of this verse are very critical for a genuine practitioner. The eight mundane concerns are attitudes that tend to dominate our lives generally. They are: becoming elated when someone praises you, becoming depressed when someone insults or belittles you, feeling happy when you experience success, being depressed

~

when you experience failure, being joyful when
you acquire wealth, feeling dispirited when you
become poor, being pleased when you have fame,
and feeling depressed when you lack recognition.

~

~

A true practitioner should ensure that his or her cultivation of altruism is not defiled by these thoughts. For example, if, as I am giving this talk, I have even the slightest thought in the back of my mind that I hope people admire me, then that indicates that my motivation is defiled by mundane considerations, or what the Tibetans call the 'eight mundane concerns.' It is very important to check oneself and ensure that is not the case. Similarly, a practitioner may apply altruistic ideals in his daily life, but if all of a sudden he feels proud about it and thinks, 'Ah, I'm a great practitioner,' immediately the eight mundane concerns defile his practice. The same applies if a practitioner thinks,

~

'I hope people admire what I'm doing,' expecting to receive praise for the great effort he is making. All these are mundane concerns that spoil one's practice, and it is important to ensure that this does not happen so we keep our practice pure.

~

~

As you can see, the instructions that you can find in the *lo-jong* teachings on transforming the mind are very powerful. They really make you think. For example there is a passage which says:

May I be gladdened when someone belittles me, and may I not take pleasure when someone praises me. If I do take pleasure in praise then it immediately increases my arrogance, pride, and conceit; whereas if I take pleasure in criticism, then at least it will open my eyes to my own shortcomings.

This is indeed a powerful sentiment.

~

Up to this point we have discussed all the practices that are related to the cultivation of what is known as 'conventional bodhichitta,' the altruistic intention to become fully enlightened for the benefit of all sentient beings. Now, the last two lines of the Eight Verses relate to the practice of cultivating what is known as 'ultimate bodhichitta,' which refers to the development of insight into the ultimate nature of reality. Although the generation of wisdom is part of the bodhisattva ideal, as embodied in the six perfections, generally speaking, as we saw earlier, there are two main aspects to the Buddhist path – method and wisdom. Both are included in the definition of enlightenment, which

~

is the non-duality of perfected form and perfected wisdom. The practice of wisdom or insight correlates with the perfection of wisdom, while the practice of skillful means or methods correlates with the perfection of form.

~

~

The Buddhist path is presented within a general framework of what are called Ground, Path, and Fruition. First, we develop an understanding of the basic nature of reality in terms of two levels of reality, the conventional truth and the ultimate truth; this is the ground. Then, on the actual path, we gradually embody meditation and spiritual practice as a whole in terms of method and wisdom. The final fruition of one's spiritual path takes place in terms of the non-duality of perfected form and perfected wisdom.

~

~

The last two lines read:

And may I, recognizing all things as illusion,
Devoid of clinging, be released from bondage.

These lines actually point to the practice of cultivating insight into the nature of reality, but on the surface they seem to denote a way of relating to the world during the stages of post-meditation. In the Buddhist teachings on the ultimate nature of reality, two significant time periods are distinguished; one is the actual meditative session during which you remain in single-pointed meditation, and the other is the period subsequent

~

to the meditative session when you engage actively with the real world, as it were. So, here, these two lines directly concern the way of relating to the world in the aftermath of one's meditation. This is why the text speaks of appreciating the illusion-like nature of reality, because this is the way one perceives things when one arises from single-pointed meditation.

~

~

In my view, these lines make a very important point because sometimes people have the idea that what really matters is single-pointed meditation within the meditative session. They pay much less attention to how this experience should be applied in post-meditation periods. However, I think the post-meditation period is very important. The whole point of meditating on the ultimate nature of reality is to ensure that you are not fooled by appearances, and that you appreciate the gap between how things appear to you and how they really are. Buddhism explains that appearances can often be deluding. With a deeper understanding of reality, you can go beyond appearances and

~

relate to the world in a much more appropriate, effective, and realistic manner.

~

~

I often give the example of how we should relate to our neighbors. Imagine that you are living in a particular part of town where interaction with your neighbors is almost impossible, and yet it is actually better if you do interact with them rather than ignore them. To do so in the wisest way depends on how well you understand your neighbors' personality. If, for example, the man living next door is very resourceful, then being friendly and communicating with him will be to your benefit. At the same time, if you know that deep down he can also be quite tricky, that knowledge is invaluable if you are to maintain a cordial relationship and be vigilant so that he does not take

~

advantage of you. Likewise, once you have a deeper understanding of the nature of reality, then in post-meditation, when you actually engage with the world, you will relate to people and things in a much more appropriate and realistic manner.

~

~

THE EIGHT VERSES ON TRANSFORMING THE MIND

With a determination to achieve the highest aim

For the benefit of all sentient beings,

Which surpasses even the wish-fulfilling gem,

May I hold them dear at all times.

Whenever I interact with someone,

May I view myself as the lowest amongst all,

And, from the very depths of my heart,

Respectfully hold others as superior.

~

~

In all my deeds may I probe into my mind,

And as soon as mental and emotional afflictions arise –

As they endanger myself and others –

May I strongly confront them and avert them.

When I see beings of unpleasant character

Oppressed by strong negativity and suffering,

May I hold them dear – for they are rare to find –

As if I have discovered a jewel treasure!

When others, out of jealously

Treat me wrongly with abuse, slander, and scorn,

May I take upon myself the defeat

And offer to others the victory.

~

When someone whom I have helped,

Or in whom I have placed great hopes,

Mistreats me in extremely hurtful ways,

May I regard him still as my precious teacher.

In brief, may I offer benefit and joy

To all my mothers, both directly and indirectly,

May I quietly take upon myself

All hurts and pains of my mothers.

May all this remain undefiled

By the stains of the eight mundane concerns;

And may I, recognizing all things as illusion,

Devoid of clinging, be released from bondage.

~

GENERATING THE MIND
FOR ENLIGHTENMENT

For those who admire the spiritual ideals of the Eight Verses on Transforming the Mind it is helpful to recite the following verses for generating the mind for enlightenment. Practicing Buddhists should recite the verses and reflect upon the meaning of the words, while trying to enhance their altruism and compassion. Those of you who are practitioners of other religious traditions can draw from your own spiritual teachings, and try to commit yourselves to cultivating altruistic thoughts in pursuit of the altruistic ideal.

~

With a wish to free all beings
I shall always go for refuge
to the Buddha, Dharma and Sangha
until I reach full enlightenment.

Enthused by wisdom and compassion,
today in the Buddha's presence
I generate the Mind for Full Awakening
for the benefit of all sentient beings.

As long as space endures,
as long as sentient beings remain,
until then, may I too remain
and dispel the miseries of the world.

~

In conclusion, those who, like myself, consider themselves to be followers of Buddha, should practice as much as we can. To followers of other religious traditions, I would like to say, 'Please practice your own religion seriously and sincerely.' And to non-believers, I request you to try to be warm-hearted. I ask this of you because these mental attitudes actually bring us happiness. As I have mentioned before, taking care of others actually benefits you.

Continuing on this path, you will also begin to appreciate the value of human life, how precious it is, and the fact that as human beings we are capable of reflecting on these questions and

~

following a spiritual practice. Then you will really appreciate a point emphasized again and again by many great Tibetan masters: that we should not waste the opportunity offered to us in this life, because human life is so precious and so difficult to achieve. As life is valuable it is important to do something meaningful with it right now, since, by its very nature, it is also transient. This shows how you can bring all the elements of the various spiritual practices together so that they have a cumulative effect on your daily practice.

~